Vermont

Niels R. Jensen

Visit us at
www.abdopublishing.com

Published by ABDO Publishing Company, 8000 West 78th Street, Suite 310, Edina, Minnesota 55439 USA. Copyright ©2010 by Abdo Consulting Group, Inc. International copyrights reserved in all countries. No part of this book may be reproduced in any form without written permission from the publisher. The Checkerboard Library™ is a trademark and logo of ABDO Publishing Company.

Printed in the United States.

Editor: John Hamilton
Graphic Design: Sue Hamilton
Cover Illustration: Neil Klinepier
Cover Photo: iStock Photo
Interior Photo Credits: Adair Mulligan, Alamy, AP Images, Corbis, Getty, Granger Collection, iStock Photo, Jupiterimages, Library of Congress, Mile High Maps, Mountain High Maps, North Wind Picture Archives, One Mile Up, PhotoResearchers, Sandra Mansi, Trapp Family Lodge-Stowe,VT, U.S. Fish and Wildlife, Vermont Historical Society, and Woodstock Historical Society.
Statistics: State population statistics taken from 2008 U.S. Census Bureau estimates. City and town population statistics taken from July 1, 2007, U.S. Census Bureau estimates. Land and water area statistics taken from 2000 Census, U.S. Census Bureau.

Manufactured with paper containing at least 10% post-consumer waste

Library of Congress Cataloging-in-Publication Data

Jensen, Niels R., 1949-
  Vermont / Niels R. Jensen.
      p. cm. -- (The United States)
  Includes index.
  ISBN 978-1-60453-681-2
  1. Vermont--Juvenile literature. I. Title.

F49.3.J46 2009
974.3--dc22
                                    2008052879

Table of Contents

Green Mountain State

Vermont is full of beautiful mountains, fertile valleys, and large lakes. It is a place where people come year-round to enjoy the great outdoors. The word "Vermont" is a combination of two French words (*verts monts*) that mean "green mountains."

Vermont has a long history of independent thought. When outsiders claimed the region, the people declared themselves free and independent. People's individual rights remain very important in the state today.

Farming and manufacturing have long been important to Vermont's economy. Both have changed over the years. Today, most farms make dairy products, and much of the farmland has gone back to woodlands. Tourism is also very important to the state.

Vermont is a state filled with beautiful woodlands and farms.

Quick Facts

Name: Vermont is French (*verts monts*) for "green mountains."

State Capital: Montpelier, population 7,806

Date of Statehood: March 4, 1791 (14th state)

Population: 621,270 (49th-most populous state)

Area (Total Land and Water): 9,614 square miles (24,900 sq km), 45th-largest state

Largest City: Burlington, population 38,531

Nickname: Green Mountain State

Motto: Freedom and Unity

State Bird: Hermit Thrush

Red Clover

Granite

Sugar Maple

Mt. Mansfield

Chester Arthur

Calvin Coolidge

State Flower: Red Clover

State Rock: Granite, Marble, and Slate

State Tree: Sugar Maple

State Song: "These Green Mountains"

Highest Point: Mt. Mansfield, 4,393 ft (1,339 m)

Lowest Point: Lake Champlain, 95 ft (29 m)

Average July Temperature: 68°F (20°C)

Record High Temperature: 105°F (41°C) in Vernon, July 4, 1911

Average January Temperature: 17°F (-8°C)

Record Low Temperature: -50°F (-46°C) in Bloomfield, December 30, 1933

Average Annual Precipitation: 40 inches (102 cm)

Number of U.S. Senators: 2

Number of U.S. Representatives: 1

U.S. Presidents Born In State: Chester A. Arthur (1881-1885), Calvin Coolidge (1923-1929)

U.S. Postal Service Abbreviation: VT

Geography

Vermont is the only state in New England that does not touch the Atlantic Ocean. It shares an international border with Canada.

Vermont's mountains are very old. They are part of the Appalachian Mountains, which reach 1,500 miles (2,414 km) from Canada to Alabama. They were pushed up more than 400 million years ago.

During the last ice age, glaciers one-mile (1.6-km) thick covered Vermont. The ice shaped the mountains, scraped out valleys, and created lakes. The last glaciers melted about 10,000 years ago.

The western side of Vermont includes the Taconic Mountains and the Champlain Lowlands. There is fertile soil in the lowlands, which is good for farming.

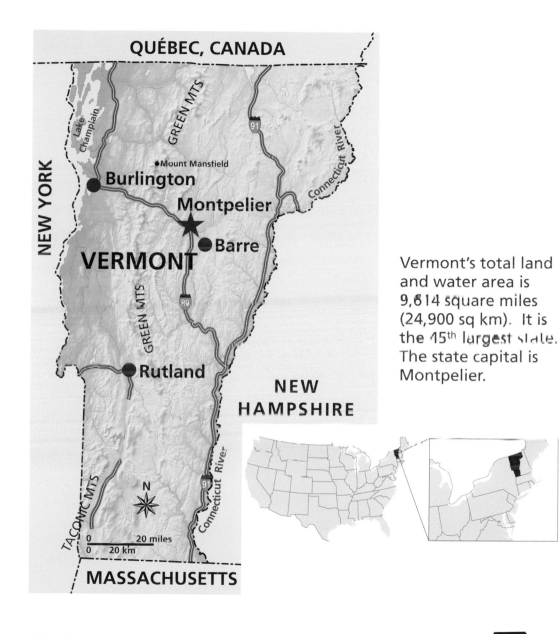

QUÉBEC, CANADA

GREEN MTS

Lake Champlain

•Mount Mansfield

●Burlington

NEW YORK

Montpelier

★

●Barre

VERMONT

GREEN MTS

●Rutland

Connecticut River

**NEW
HAMPSHIRE**

TACONIC MTS

N

0   20 miles
0   20 km

Connecticut River

MASSACHUSETTS

Vermont's total land
and water area is
9,614 square miles
(24,900 sq km). It is
the 15th largest state.
The state capital is
Montpelier.

Lake Champlain is also on the western side of Vermont. It is one of the largest lakes in the United States.

The Green Mountains run north and south through the middle of the state. They were named the Green Mountains because of their green forests, and because of the region's green-colored rocks. Vermont's highest mountain is Mt. Mansfield. It is in the north part of the Green Mountains. It is 4,393 feet (1,339 m) high.

The eastern foothills region of the Green Mountains has rolling hills and valleys. There are also some granite mountains. The south-flowing Connecticut River runs along the border of New Hampshire to the east.

The highlands in the northeast part of the state are known as the Northeast Kingdom. This rugged region has mountains, forests, bogs, and swamps.

Lake Champlain was named after the French explorer Samuel de Champlain. He found the lake in 1609. The lake lies between the Green Mountains of Vermont and the Adirondack Mountains of New York State. Much of the area surrounding the lake is farmland.

Climate and Weather

Vermont has a humid continental climate. There are warm summers, cold winters, and large swings in temperature.

Different air masses come into the state. Warm, moist air arrives from the south. Cold, dry air blows in from the north. Cool, damp air comes from the east, blowing in from the Atlantic Ocean.

A Vermont skier smiles as he faces below-zero temperatures.

Severe weather can sometimes hit Vermont. The state can have blizzards, freezing rains, tornados, and heavy thunderstorms. The northern part of Vermont is colder, and gets a lot of winter snow.

People often talk about Vermont's "mud season." It is a time in late winter and early spring when the melting snow is unable to soak into the frozen ground. It makes the dirt roads and trails so muddy that cars may get stuck.

A horse is rescued after becoming trapped during Vermont's mud season.

Plants and Animals

Vermont is famous for its stunning fall colors, when tree leaves turn vivid shades of red, yellow, and orange. The state's forests cover about 4.6 million acres (1.9 million ha). This is about 75 percent of the state's land. The local trees include alder, ash, aspen, basswood, beech, birch, butternut, cedar, cherry, oak, pine, tamarack, tupelo, and spruce. The sugar maple is the state tree.

Trout

The streams, rivers, and lakes of Vermont have a lot of fish. There are about 90 species swimming in the state's waters. They include bass, perch, pike, salmon, smelt, trout, walleye, and bullhead.

A white horse stands in a field surrounded by the beautiful fall colors of Vermont's trees.

Vermont is home to plentiful wildlife, including white-tailed deer, beaver, black bear, bobcat, coyote, fisher, fox, mink, moose, muskrat, otter, raccoon, skunk, and snowshoe hare.

Birds that nest in Vermont include duck, goose, ruffled grouse, gull, owl, swan, hawk, heron, tern, turkey, and many others. In recent years, there has been a recovery of bald eagles, peregrine falcons, ospreys, and loons in Vermont. Their numbers had declined because of widespread use of DDT and other insecticides. DDT was banned in the United States in 1972.

Loons have made a comeback in the state of Vermont in recent years.

Eastern coyotes first appeared in Vermont in the 1940s.

Moose

Red Fox

Snowshoe Hare

People have lived in the Vermont area for at least 10,000 years. Early Native American tribes in the area were mostly Iroquois and an Algonquin group called the Abenaki.

The first European explorer in the area was Jacques Cartier. He was a Frenchman who sailed up the St. Lawrence River in 1535. Another Frenchman, Samuel de Champlain, came in 1609. He claimed the area for France. Lake Champlain is named after him.

In 1609, Samuel de Champlain, along with Algonquin Native American allies, fought the Iroquois near Lake Champlain.

In 1690, people from New York set
up a trading post at Chimney Point,
in northwestern Vermont. The British
built Fort Dummer in southeastern

Fort Dummer was
built in 1724.

Vermont in 1724. It was the first permanent European
settlement in the state.

The French built powerful forts near Lake Champlain.

King George III
was awarded all
of the French
land east of the
Mississippi River
in the 1763 Treaty
of Paris.

Conflicts between the British and
French caused the French and Indian
War (1754-1763). Both sides wanted
to control Lake Champlain and its
waterways, which were important for
trade. After much fighting, the 1763
Treaty of Paris awarded the British
all of the French land east of the
Mississippi River, including Vermont.

On May 10, 1775, Ethan Allen and the Green Mountain Boys captured Fort Ticonderoga. No one on either side was killed in the taking of the fort. Captain William Delaplace, the fort's commander, surrendered his sword. The troops captured cannons and other heavy weapons, which the American forces needed.

After the war, New York and New Hampshire both wanted Vermont land. The people of Vermont resisted. They formed a powerful militia called the Green Mountain Boys in the 1760s to protect Vermont. In 1775, during the Revolutionary War (1775-1783), the Green Mountain Boys and New York troops captured British Fort Ticonderoga, near the south end of Lake Champlain.

In 1777, Vermont declared itself independent. It called itself the Vermont Republic. Its state constitution was the first to

Old Constitution House is where the Vermont Republic began.

give voting rights to all men, outlaw slavery, and give public money for education. The Vermont Republic joined the United States in 1791. It was the first state to join the Union after the original 13 colonies.

In September 1814, the American fleet defeated British warships on Lake Champlain in the Battle of Plattsburgh.

During the War of 1812 (1812-1815), British and American warships fought on Lake Champlain. The American fleet defeated the British at the Battle of Plattsburgh in 1814.

Vermont saw a growth in farming and manufacturing in the mid-1800s. The first railway was built in 1848. Most Vermont citizens opposed slavery. The Underground Railroad was active in the state. During the Civil War (1861-1865), about 34,000 people from Vermont fought for the Union.

In the 1900s, dairy farming was an important industry in Vermont.

There were many changes in Vermont during the 1900s. Manufacturing became more important. Less land was used for farming, although dairying remained strong. The Great Depression of the 1930s hit Vermont hard. Many people lost their jobs. During America's involvement in World War II (1941-1945), more than 50,000 people from Vermont served in the armed forces. After the war, service industries became much more important to the state's economy, especially tourism. Today, ski resorts bring many visitors to the state each year.

Did You Know?

- In 1927, a major flood in Vermont killed about 85 people and destroyed many homes, roads, and bridges. The state of Vermont and the United States government helped people rebuild.

- *The Sound of Music* features the Trapp family of Austria. The Trapps moved to Vermont in the early 1940s. Today, surviving family members run the Trapp Family Lodge, a resort near Stowe.

- According to Abenaki and Iroquois legends, there is a monster living in Lake Champlain. Sightings have been reported for years, but none are proven. The monster's nickname is Champ.

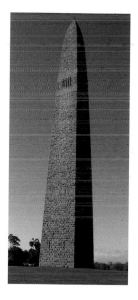

- Bennington Battle Day is a Vermont state holiday. It celebrates an important American victory during the Revolutionary War in 1777. American soldiers, along with many of Vermont's Green Mountain Boys militia, defeated an invading force of British troops. A 300-foot (91-m) monument has been built to remember this battle.

People

Ethan Allen (1738-1789) was an early Vermont frontiersman and soldier. He was born in Connecticut, but moved to the Vermont area after the French and Indian War. He led the militia group known as the Green Mountain Boys. In 1775, during the Revolutionary War, he helped lead soldiers who captured Fort Ticonderoga, a British stronghold near Lake Champlain. It was one of the first important victories of the Revolutionary War. Later that year, Allen was captured during an attack on Montreal, Canada. He was released in 1778. He returned home, where he worked to achieve statehood for Vermont.

John Deere (1804-1886) was a blacksmith, inventor, and maker of farm equipment. He invented a self-cleaning steel plow that was tough and efficient enough to handle the prairie sod of America's Great

Plains. He started Deere and Company in 1868. Today it remains one of the largest companies in the United States. Deere was born in Rutland, Vermont.

George Dewey (1837-1917) was an officer of the U.S. Navy. He commanded American ships during the Spanish-American War of 1898. He is famous for his victory at the Battle of Manila Bay, in the Philippines. The battle was won without a single American combat death. Dewey was later promoted to Admiral of the Navy, the service's highest rank. No one else has ever held such a high rank in the U.S. Navy. Dewey was born in Montpelier, Vermont.

Elisha Graves Otis (1811-1861) invented the first automatic elevator brake. It kept an elevator from falling if the cables holding it broke. His safety device made modern skyscrapers possible. The Otis Elevator Company is still in business today. Otis was born in Halifax, Vermont.

Joseph Smith

Brigham Young

Joseph Smith (1805-1844) and **Brigham Young** (1801-1877) were early leaders of the Church of Jesus Christ of Latter-day Saints. Joseph Smith was born in Sharon, Vermont. Brigham Young was born in Whitingham, Vermont. The church's followers are called Mormons. Smith organized the church in 1830. In 1847, Young led a group of Mormon pioneers to Salt Lake Valley, Utah Territory. He later became Utah's first governor.

Cities

Burlington is the largest city in Vermont. It is located on the eastern shore of Lake Champlain. Its population is 38,531. However, the neighboring cities of South Burlington, Winooski, and Essex make the total metropolitan area much larger. Education and health services are important to Burlington's economy. The city is home to the University of Vermont, Burlington College, and Champlain College. There is also a campus of the Community College of Vermont in Burlington. Ben & Jerry's ice cream got its start in Burlington in 1978.

Rutland is in the south-central part of Vermont. Its population is 16,826. In the late-1800s, the city was one of the world's largest producers of marble. Today's businesses include aircraft parts manufacturing, mineral production, and consumer credit reporting. The city has many houses on the National Register of Historic Places. The Vermont State Fair is held in Rutland each September.

Barre is in the north-central part of Vermont. Its population is 8,905. The city is famous for its granite production, which is used for tombstones, monuments, buildings, and kitchen counters.

A granite statue of Scottish poet Robert Burns stands in Barre.

Montpelier is the capital of Vermont. It population is 7,806. It is the smallest state capital in the United States. The city's main employer is the state government. There are also insurance companies, as well as some granite processing. The Vermont College of Fine Arts is located in Montpelier.

The state capitol in Montpelier.

Transportation

There are more than 14,000 miles (22,531 km) of roads and about 2,700 bridges in Vermont. The state's major interstate highways include I-89, I-91 and I-93. They each run mainly in a north-and-south direction. Several car ferries operate on Lake Champlain.

Vermont is famous for its many wooden, covered bridges. There are about 100 remaining in the state.

At 460 feet (140 m), the Windsor-Cornish Bridge between Windsor, Vermont, and Cornish, New Hampshire, was the country's longest covered bridge until 2008.

Two Amtrak passenger trains serve Vermont. The *Ethan Allen Express* reaches Rutland and Fair Haven from New York. The *Vermonter* runs from Washington,

The Amtrak *Vermonter* heads down the tracks in Middlesex, Vermont.

D.C., to St. Albans, Vermont, through Montpelier. There are nine railroads providing freight services.

Vermont's main commercial airport is Burlington International Airport. It is also used by the Vermont Air National Guard.

Natural Resources

Forests cover about 75 percent of Vermont. The state's forests support logging, furniture making, and outdoor recreation. The state is the largest producer of pure maple syrup in the United States. Nearly half a million gallons (1.9 million liters) is produced each year.

Sap is collected from a maple tree.

The value of Vermont's agriculture is about $674 million annually. The state ranks 41st in the nation. There are about 7,000 farms in Vermont, with an average size of 177 acres (72 ha). Nearly 75 percent of the state's farm products involve dairy, such as milk, cheese, butter, and yogurt.

Vermont's apple varieties include Cortland, Empire, McIntosh, and Red Delicious. Some apples are used to make cider and applesauce.

Vermont is the largest center of marble and granite quarrying in the country. Slate is also quarried.

A granite quarry in Barre, Vermont.

Industry

About 1 of every 10 Vermont jobs is related to tourism. People come to the state to experience the outdoors, see stunning fall colors, or visit a farm. Vermont has 53 state parks. Part of the famous Appalachian Trail follows the Green Mountains.

Vermont is very beautiful in winter. Popular ski resorts include Stowe Mountain, Sugarbush, Smugglers' Notch, and Killington.

Many ski competitions are held at popular Vermont resorts, such as Stowe Mountain.

Ice cream maker Ben & Jerry's factory tour in Waterbury, Vermont, is one of the most popular stops for visitors.

Vermont is home to Burton Snowboards. Orvis is a sporting equipment and clothing business based in the state. Ben & Jerry's and Bruegger's Bagels are among Vermont's food products companies.

Vermont has many financial services companies, furniture makers, insurance companies, medical facilities, retail centers, and technology businesses. IBM has a large manufacturing plant at Essex Junction.

Sports

Vermont is well known for its winter sports. It is a favorite destination for skiers and snowboarders. Some ski areas host national and international competitions.

First ski tow rope.

The country's first tow rope for skiers was made in Woodstock, Vermont, in 1934. The back wheel of a jacked-up Ford Model A automobile supplied the power. Today, Vermont's skiing industry brings in more than $750 million yearly to the state.

Vermont also has many summer outdoor activities. Popular sports include golfing, biking, hiking, rock climbing, water sports, hunting, and fishing.

There are no major league sports teams in Vermont. The Vermont Lake Monsters are a popular minor league baseball team. There are also several minor league basketball, football, and soccer teams. College and high school sports are also popular in Vermont.

"Champ," the mascot for the Vermont Lake Monsters, cheers on the popular team.

Entertainment

Vermont has several museums and historic sites. They include the Ethan Allen Homestead Museum near Burlington, and the boyhood home of President Calvin Coolidge, in Plymouth Notch. The Marsh-Billings-Rockefeller National Historical Park, near Woodstock, has scientifically managed forests and farmlands.

The Vermont Theatre Company holds an annual Shakespeare festival. It also offers children's theater performances.

Young actors perform a Shakespeare play.

The Vermont Symphony Orchestra Association performs throughout the state. The Vermont Mozart Festival features great musicians from around the world.

There are many popular festivals in the state. They include the Green Mountain Film Festival, Vermont Maple Festival, Vermont Apple Festival, and Middlebury Festival on the Green.

The Vermont State Fair is held at Rutland. About 85,000 people visit the annual 10-day agriculture and entertainment event.

The Ring of Fire is enjoyed by riders at the Vermont State Fair.

Timeline

Pre-1500s—Abenaki and Iroquois Native Americans inhabit the Vermont area.

1609—Explorer Samuel de Champlain claims Vermont area for France.

1724—The British build Fort Dummer, the first permanent European settlement in Vermont.

1763—British gain control of Vermont area after the French and Indian War.

1775—Vermont militia Green Mountain Boys capture Fort Ticonderoga.

1791—Vermont becomes the 14th state of the United States.

1861-1865—About 34,000 people from Vermont serve in the Civil War.

1927—Major flooding causes many deaths and destruction.

1930s—Tourism starts to become an important industry for Vermont.

1941-1945—More than 50,000 people from Vermont serve in World War II.

2004—Popular six-term Vermont Governor Howard Dean runs for president, but is unsuccessful.

Glossary

Covered Bridges—Usually made of wood, covered bridges have enclosed sides and a roof, which greatly protect the structure. Some are strong enough to support trains.

Glacier—Immense sheets of ice that grow and shrink as the climate changes. Glaciers carve and shape the land beneath them.

Great Depression—A time in American history beginning in 1929 and lasting for several years when many businesses failed and millions of people lost their jobs.

Insecticides—Chemicals used to kill mosquitoes and other insects. The insecticide DDT was used in the United States from the 1940s until it was banned in 1972. DDT is poisonous to people and animals.

Iroquois—A powerful alliance of Native American tribes,

including the Cayuga, Mohawk, Oneida, Onondaga, Seneca, and Tuscarora people.

Lake Champlain—A large lake that lies between Vermont and New York. It is about 110 miles (177 km) long, and covers 435 square miles (1,127 sq km).

Marble—A rock that is prized for sculptures, monuments, and buildings. It is a type of limestone.

Militia—A group of people who perform part-time military duties. Instead of serving full-time, they are called up for service when needed.

Revolutionary War—The war fought between the American colonies and Great Britain from 1775-1783. It is also known as the War of Independence or the American Revolution.

Underground Railroad—Not an actual railroad, but a system of safe houses and connecting routes used to help African Americans escape from Southern slave states.

Index